Good morning! When I wake up ...

I eat a free-range egg for my breakfast.

Hens that live outdoors have more space and a healthier diet than hens kept in cages. This means free-range eggs are better for you.

I put my eggshell
in the compost bin ...

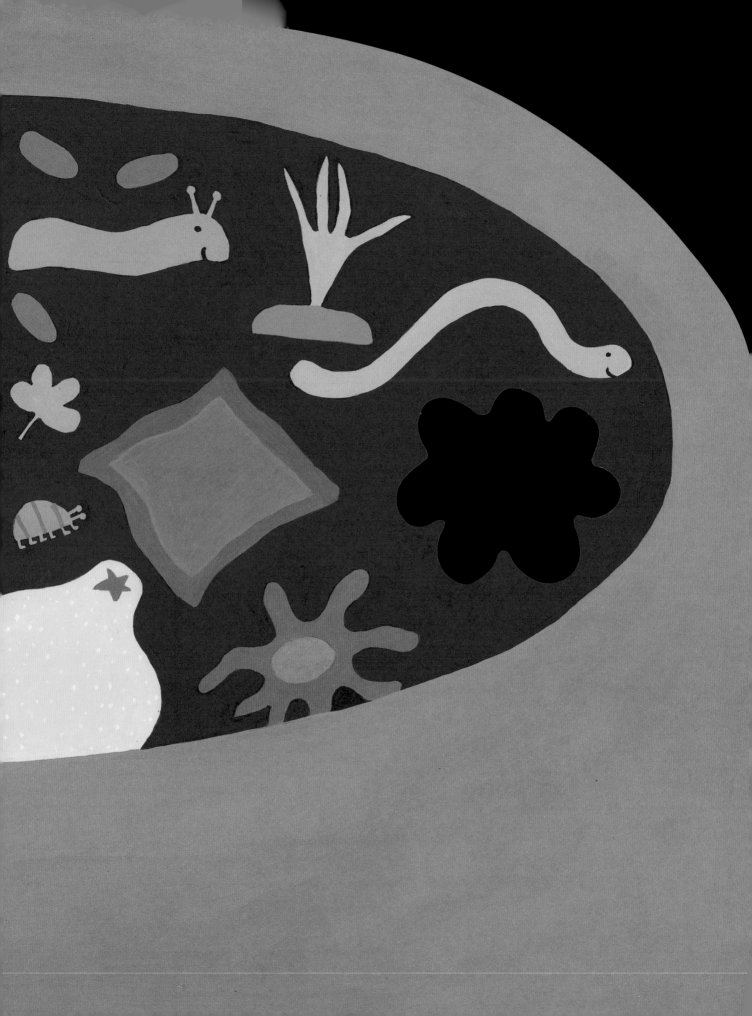

Some household waste is biodegradable. Composting it means less rubbish goes to landfill sites.

where it turns into
soil for growing vegetables.

I help empty the washing machine ...

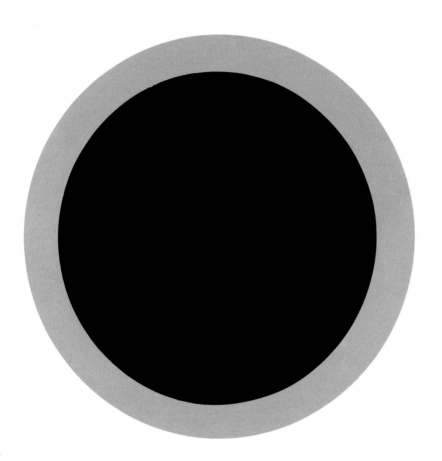

A tumble-dryer is more energy-intensive than any other household appliance. Drying clothes on a washing line uses only free natural

and peg our clothes out to dry.

At school ...

Making a toy out of old material is fun and a great way to recycle.

At lunch ...

I make presents
for my grandma.

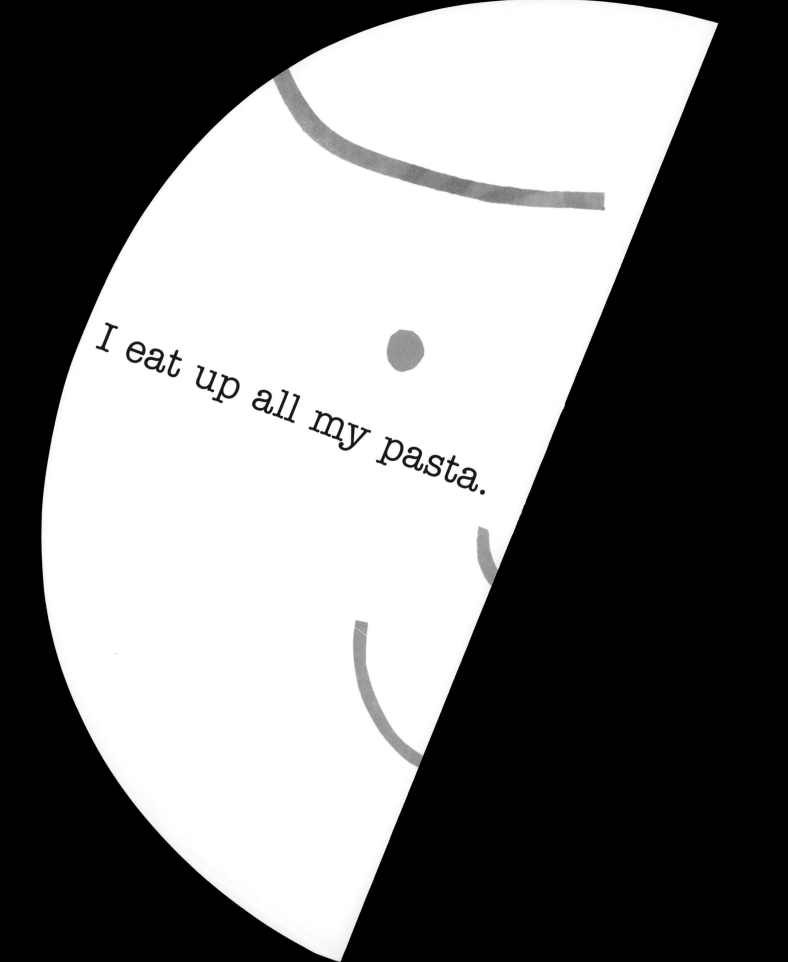

I eat up all my pasta.

We throw away one third of all the food we buy. If we bought only the food we actually needed to eat, we wouldn't have to grow or transport so much food, which saves lots of energy.

flour

HONEY

After school, mummy and I go to the shops ...

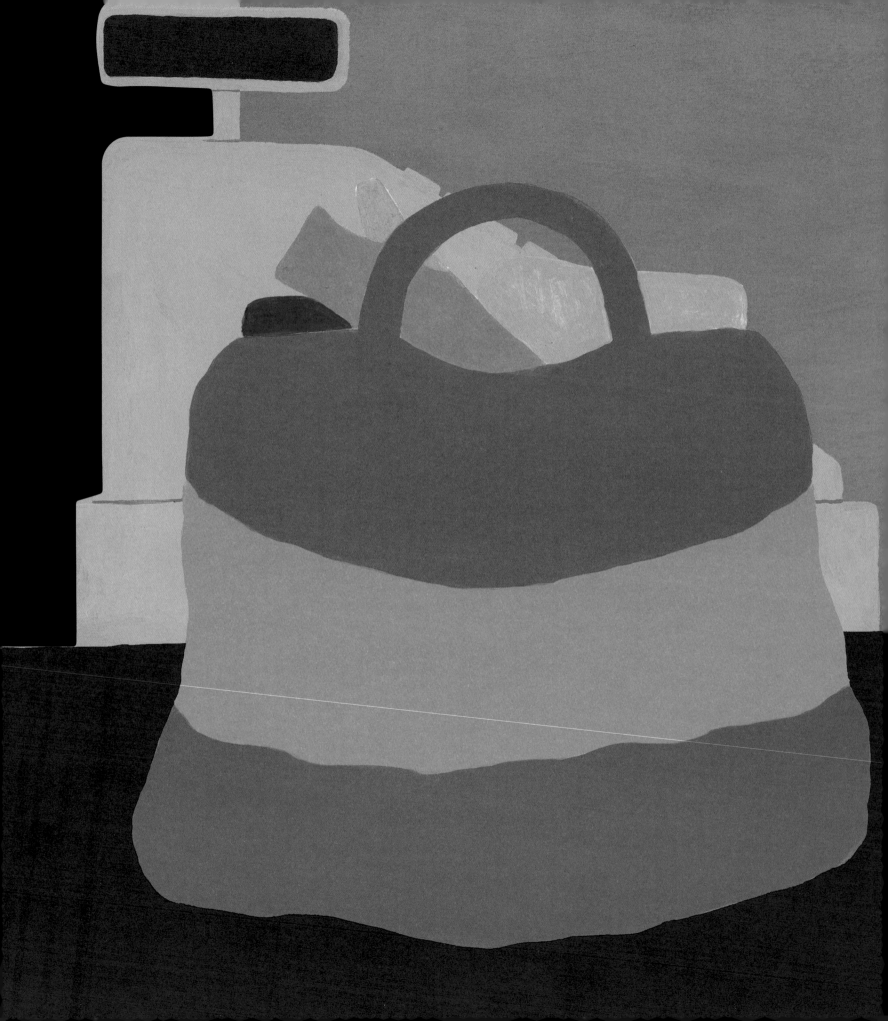

and use our own bags
to pack the shopping.

Cloth bags can be used again and again. You'll never need to use another plastic bag.

In the park ...

I play hide and seek
in the trees.

Playing outside with friends keeps you fit and makes you feel good.

flour

Daddy and I ...

PUMPKIN
SEEDS

HONEY

my
yummy
cook book

Home-made food doesn't need to contain extra ingredients such as

colourings and preservatives, so it is better for you.

Bought food is also often heavily packaged,

which is a source of unnecessary waste.

bake delicious muffins for tea.

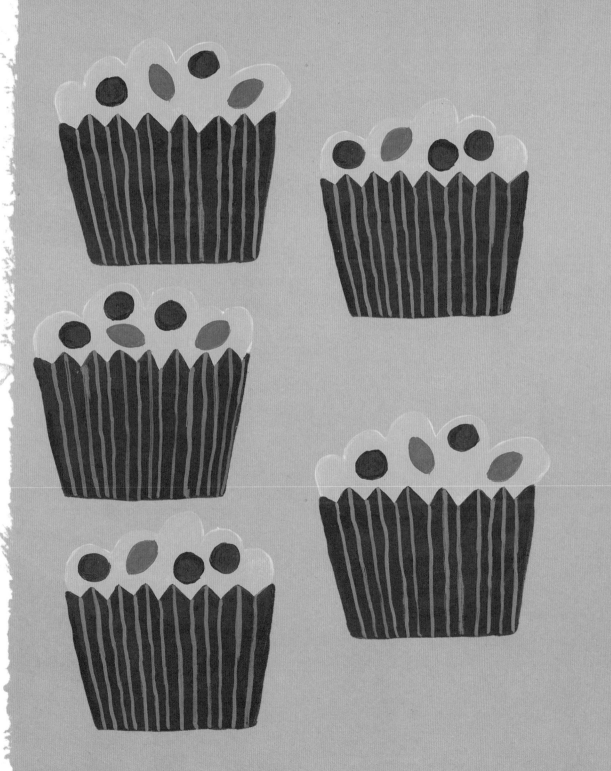

In the evening ...

You can save money and energy by not putting on the central heating until you really need to.

I put on a jumper
when I get chilly.

I have a shower before I go to bed ...

You can reduce the amount of water you use by only showering for three or four minutes.

and that's the end of my green day.